Obsessive Compulsive Personality Disorder: The Ultimate Guide to Symptoms, Treatment and Prevention

By: Clayton Geoffreys

Table of Contents

Disclaimer

This book is not intended as a substitute for the medical advice of a psychologist, physician, or medical professional. The reader should regularly visit a doctor or therapist in matters relating to his or her health and particularly with respect to symptoms that may require medical diagnosis or attention.

Foreword

Personality disorders can significantly alter the way one lives their life. Understanding the symptoms of these disorders is important for everyone. Whether or not you personally suffer from these disorders, learning to recognize symptoms is the first step to being able to best assist someone who may be suffering from a condition. Psychologists have studied disorders for many years, creating multiple iterations of diagnosis tools; it's difficult to truly pinpoint everything with 100% accuracy, but with time and further research, we as a society will become better aware of the nature of these disorders. Hopefully from reading *Obsessive Compulsive Personality Disorder: The Ultimate Guide to Symptoms, Treatment and Prevention* I can pass along some of the abundance of information I have learned about Obsessive Compulsive Personality disorder, including its symptoms, therapies to consider, and ways to begin overcoming Obsessive Compulsive Personality Disorder. Thank you for downloading my book. Hope you enjoy and if you do, please do not forget to leave a review! Also, check out my website at claytongeoffreys.com to join my exclusive list where I let you know about my latest books. To thank you for your purchase, you can go to my site to download a free copy of *33 Life Lessons: Success Principles, Career Advice & Habits of Successful People*. In the book, you'll learn from some of the greatest thought leaders of different industries on what it takes to become successful and how to live a great life.

Cheers,

Clayton Geoffreys

What is Obsessive Compulsive Personality Disorder?

Personality disorders are characterized by certain patterns of behavior that are not functional in the context of the society wherein the individual operates. These traits must have a negative impact on the personal and social aspects of an individual's life to be classified as a personality disorder. Obsessive Compulsive Personality Disorder (OCPD) is one such disorder. OCPD is generally defined as a preoccupation with the strict compliance of rigid guidelines and rules of behavior. It affects about 1 in every 100 people and is diagnosed twice as often in males as compared to females. OCPD usually becomes noticeable in early adulthood but it may be developed starting in early childhood to late adolescence.

OCPD is commonly confused with Obsessive Compulsive Disorder (OCD) due to the similarities in both names and symptoms. However, there are critical differences between OCPD and OCD that distinguishes the former from the latter. For example, an OCD patient is usually aware that the symptoms of their disorder are irrational, whereas those with OCPD often do not. In fact, while an OCD patient often feels a sense of guilt for the difficulties their disorder places on their loved ones and acquaintances, the OCPD patient often sees no problem with their behavior. Rather, OCPD patients believe that other people must conform to their ideas and practices as they do things the 'correct' way.

Another difference between people with OCD and OCPD is the self-imposed rituals and regulations of those with OCD. Usually, OCD patients have unique and nonsensical actions which they feel must be completed lest something bad should happen. On the other hand, OCPD patients are more focused on completing real-world tasks in an extremely formalized and disciplined manner. This is to the extent that flexibility and productivity are sacrificed.

One of the most dominant characteristics of OCPD is a strict adherence to established rules and procedures. OCPD patients follow guidelines and regulations exactly as dictated even if it means the loss of efficiency or flexibility. People with OCPD believe that choosing to disregard the rules put in place is the 'incorrect' way of doing thing. They will not even consider breaking established rules even if those rules are difficult or complicated. Streamlining a process in a manner which deviates from the established norm is not in the nature of a person with OCPD. Moreover, an attempt to circumvent the provided instructions or regulations will cause severe cases of anxiety and potentially generate anger in the OCPD patient.

The OCPD patient has a deep need for organization and order. These individuals are likely to be very compartmentalized and cannot function properly in the chaos of a messy atmosphere. Their desks are likely to be clear of debris or personal mementos and to be military neat. This tendency is shown not just in an organized work space. The home of an OCPD patient is likely to be strictly regimented and systematized. People with OCPD are likely to enforce their need for a tightly controlled environment on those they love. The OCPD patient is likely to need every area of their home regimented, including the bedroom shared with a spouse or the children's rooms. This can generate considerable levels of stress for the family of the OCPD patient and may be responsible for high levels of tension or resentment. Family members may not understand the strict need for control that dominates the OCPD patient. However, for those suffering with OCPD, this strict regimen is more than just a preference. They have a legitimate need for order and the lack thereof can generate intolerable levels of stress for the OCPD patient.

In addition to their adherence to the status quo and their strong need for order, OCPD patients also have issues delegating responsibilities to others. People with OCPD believe that there is a strictly correct way of doing things and they have little trust in other people to perform a task in the manner they like it done. The result is an unwillingness to delegate that can cause serious problems for the OCPD patient, including overwork, late or missing projects and assignments, and high stress levels. The OCPD patient is a person who feels a strong need to control their surroundings and the outcome of a given situation. Thus, trusting others to complete important tasks is difficult for them. If a task was not completed to the standard expected by the OCPD patient, they may re-do the task to their preference without the knowledge of the others involved. This trait usually ensures that the tasks completed by an OCPD patient are done to the highest standards. However, it can also alienate those around the patient who may feel upset due to the lack of trust placed on them. Spouses may resent both the lack of confidence placed on them, and the high demands of the OCPD patient. Evidently, this may cause a strain on the relationship between the OCPD patient and their spouse.

Their strict adherence to high standards make people with OCPD excel in their careers. OCPD is unique among other disorders in such a way that the occupational function of OCPD patients themselves is unlikely to suffer. Rather, it is the potential strains in interpersonal relationships that may affect the career of OCPD patients. For example, the relationship between the OCPD patient and his or her employer may become strained if the OCPD patient believes that his or her method of completing a task is better than his or her employer's. Likewise, the lack of trust that an OCPD patient places on his or her co-workers will certainly cause difficulties. Furthermore, relationships with clients may be impeded due to the potential difficulty of working with a high-strung person, such as the OCPD patient.

The complications in relationships and the problems which arise in more personal relationships, contribute to the classification of the above-mentioned traits as a personality disorder.

The 5 Subtypes of Obsessive Compulsive Personality Disorder

Theodore Millon, an acclaimed American psychologist noted for his work on personality disorders, identified five subtypes of OCPD. These subtypes are namely, the Conscientious Compulsive, the Bureaucratic Compulsive, the Parsimonious Compulsive, the Puritanical Compulsive, and the Bedeviled Compulsive. Each subtype of OCPD has a unique set of characteristics. This allows a more individualized understanding of the OCPD patient rather than relying on the more generalized and broad diagnosis of OCPD.

The Conscientious Compulsive

The OCPD patient who falls under the conscientious compulsive subtype feels a great sense of responsibility and duty. They feel like they have an obligation to make a concerted effort in their endeavors and tend to be both solemn and diligent.

They are not the type who skips out on work or takes extended lunch breaks. Rather, they are the individuals who stay over at work (without pay) to finish a project. Likewise, they show up early for work and go home late. These individuals, like most OCPD patients, tend to follow rules religiously. These patients also tend to be inflexible in both manners and schedules. Spontaneity is not something that the conscientious compulsive feels a desire for. In fact, it is something that they distrust. They are frequently plagued with doubts and have difficulty making decisions. This can cause issues at work especially if their chosen career requires meeting tight deadlines. This OCPD subtype may strictly adhere to the rules because of a deep and abiding fear of making a mistake, or being perceived as flawed. While fear of failure is something most people struggle with, the conscientious compulsive may be driven by this fear more than the typical person.

11

The Bureaucratic Compulsive

The bureaucratic compulsive person tends to do well in formal institutions. They have narcissistic features and are disposed to being both overbearing and snobbish. Generally speaking, the bureaucratic compulsive is a nosy, meddlesome person who finds empowerment in the official rules put in place at strict organizations. They are usually unimaginative and closed minded. This lack of imagination and narrow mindedness might impede the performance of an individual in smaller companies that require greater input from their employees. However, they can excel in larger corporations or governments that require systemic output without a great deal of input. For this reason, the bureaucratic compulsive is usually found in, as their name suggests, administrative positions that allow them to succeed. Another defining feature of the bureaucratic compulsive is that they tend to define themselves in terms of group identity. The rules and norms established by the group provide the bureaucratic compulsive with a sense of security that allows him or her to build their persona within that group. Any threat to the formal or informal rules established by the group may be perceived as a threat to the OCPD patient's definition of self.

The Parsimonious Compulsive

People with OCPD that fall under the parsimonious compulsive subtype are known to have a marked tendency to hoard and to exhibit meagerly behavior. In this subtype, the items that a patient collects range from items that seemingly have no value up to items that are highly expensive. What the patient hoards is determined by the individual patient and may not make sense to others. The parsimonious compulsive person is also known be an extremely conservative individual when it comes to finances and may have been accused of being both 'tight-fisted' and 'niggardly'. However, this thriftiness is less because the patient wishes to be financially responsible but more due to their abhorrence of letting go of what is theirs. These individuals do not like to share and are often perceived as selfish. People under this subtype of OCPD are associated with schizoid features and they are afraid that other people may find out about their secret desires or impulses. They have a deep fear of loss which compels them and this fear may result in unhealthy behavior in an attempt to prevent them from experiencing the pain of such loss.

The Puritanical Compulsive

Those in the puritanical compulsive subtype of OCPD are individuals who embody the word austere. Often dogmatic, these individuals tend to be zealots in their religion and are judgmental of others who are less strict in their religious practices. Naturally, these individuals are apt to be both prudish and grim. The puritanical compulsive person is driven to be perfect and sees improper behavior (as they define it) as degrading for the individual committing those acts. For the mind of the puritanical compulsive, it is not just the behavior which must be condemned but also the person displaying such 'improper' behavior. They believe that the 'misbehaving' person should exert greater self-control and exercise better judgment. This can lead the puritanical compulsive patient to develop a bigoted attitude that alienates them from others. This alienation is compounded by the tendency of the puritanical compulsive to deny their own impulses and fantasies, particularly those which the patient finds to be distasteful or unacceptable. While these individuals are inclined to be greatly involved in their chosen religion, they can also be found working in large governments or corporations.

The Bedeviled Compulsive

OCPD patients who fall under the bedeviled compulsive subtype are perhaps the most at war with themselves. These individuals are torn between opposing viewpoints which they constantly vacillate between. This often results to the patient getting caught in a web of indecision and angst because of their fear to move forward and make a decision. The bedeviled compulsive also has an internal need to sabotage both themselves and others which contributes to their procrastination and ultimate lack of action. However, this is often hidden by their appearance of self-control which they are careful to cultivate. Evidently, with enough exposure to the patient, others will see past the façade of self-control and see the bedeviled compulsive person in a negative light. In turn, the compulsions and fixations of OCPD patients protect them from the less than fond reception they receive from others.

What Causes Obsessive Compulsive Personality Disorder?

Currently, OCPD is attributed to two causes and each cause is recognized and backed by highly recognized professionals in the field of psychology. One of the factors is biological while the other is environmental in nature. A third, less-researched factor in the development of OCPD is the psychological makeup of the patient. OCPD is unlikely to be the result of a single factor. Rather, it is the result of a combination of factors. The first, and perhaps the most researched factor in developing OCPD, is that of genetics.

In 1986, Dr. Claude Robert Cloniger, a noted American psychiatrist, introduced the theory that personality traits could be developed as a response to a genetic makeup. Dr. Cloniger specifically named three neurotransmitters (dopamine, serotonin and norepinephrine) as linked to the intensity of a person's

17

drive for seeking new experiences, avoiding pain, and reward. Dr. Cloniger proposed that an imbalance of these neurotransmitters could lead to unusual or unhealthy personality traits that, once taken as a whole, could be identified as a personality disorder.

The biological risk factor for developing obsessive compulsive personality disorder comes in the form of a dopamine genome, specifically, the polymorphism of the dopamine D3 receptor, or DRD3. Polymorphism is a natural variation in a gene, chromosome, or DNA sequence. It is a fairly common condition in the general population and typically has no effect on a person.

However, studies showed that the polymorphism of the DRD3 gene has been linked to the diagnosis of OCPD and Avoidant Personality Disorder. A multivariate study of personality disorders using twins indicated a 27% chance of OCPD being hereditarily passed. Only 11% of the variance in OCPD was accounted for by environmental factors, leading to the conclusion that OCPD is somewhat hereditary and, therefore, genetic in cause. This biological factor in the development of OCPD is a distinguishing characteristic which separates OCPD from other cluster C disorders such as Avoidant Personality Disorder and Dependent Personality Disorder.

However, this is not to say that OCPD is only caused by genetic factors. An individual may have a genetic predisposition for OCPD but this does not guarantee that the individual will, in fact, develop this disorder. Other factors play a role in the development of OCPD, including environmental and psychological factors throughout an individual's childhood and adolescence.

The exact nature of environmental factors which cause OCPD is yet to be identified. Some psychologists believe that OCPD may develop as a reaction to the experience of having too much responsibility during childhood or adolescence. This responsibility may have been placed on the child as a result of some factors which require the parents to delegate more duties to the child out of necessity. For instance, a widowed or single parent may rely on the eldest child to help raise his or her younger siblings. At times, the eldest child may even have to bring in additional income for the family. This increased reliance on the child may cause the child to over develop their sense of responsibility, which may contribute to the child's extreme need for order and high self-expectations.

Other environmental factors which contribute to the development of OCPD need not be traumatic. Parents who have extremely high expectations and place great emphasis on order and proper behavior may also contribute to the child's eventual development of OCPD. There are arguments stating that OCPD is a result of learned behavior. For instance, one study found that the parents of children with OCD were more likely to display traits of OCPD than the parents of children without OCD. While the two disorders are separate and distinct, there are similarities in symptoms. The fact that those with OCPD are linked to children with OCD showed that environmental factors play a role in acquiring obsessive-compulsive behaviors. Consequently, if the child of the OCPD patient develops OCD, then the parents of the OCPD patient could possibly be the origin of the OCPD patient's behavior.

While the biological and environmental factors were largely the focus of the psychological community, a third factor which should also be considered is the psychological tendencies of the individual themselves. The psychological makeup of a child may demonstrate susceptibility, or lack of susceptibility, toward OCPD. For instance, a child who enjoys messy and artistic hobbies is unlikely to develop OCPD. The restrictions imposed on them by the disorder would be in direct contrast to the child's intrinsic personality. Therefore, the disorder is less likely to develop. In contrast, a child who enjoys more regimented activities and has a stricter internal code of conduct may be more likely to develop OCPD. Other factors, such as a traumatic experience that dramatically alters the child's definition of self, may override these in-born psychological factors. However, in th absence of a traumatic experience, psychological factors may play a significant role in the development of OCPD, aside from genetic or environmental factors.

As previously stated, it is unlikely that a single factor would result in the development of OCPD. However, this is not to say that the development of OCPD from a single factor is impossible. It is just unlikely. Similarly, an individual with each of these factors is more likely to develop obsessive compulsive personality disorder. A person who had significant amounts of responsibility placed on them at a young age, had strict and overly organized parents, and who have a polymorphic DRD3 gene are statistically more likely to be diagnosed with OCPD than a person who lack these factors.

The 9 Most Common Symptoms of Obsessive Compulsive Personality Disorder

There are several symptoms of OCPD, not all of which may present themselves in a single patient. However, in order for a diagnosis of OCPD to be made, at least four symptoms must be present. The manifested symptoms must also be severe enough to have a significant negative impact in the social or professional life of the patient. For those with OCPD, this impact is usually felt most in interpersonal relationships, which the OCPD patient has difficulty developing and maintaining.

1. An Obsession with the Rules

The first of these symptoms is an inordinate obsession with rules, details, lists, schedules, and organization. Those with OCPD are so preoccupied with how a task is completed or its adherence to a preset schedule that sometimes they miss the point of an activity. An example of this is when a parent takes their child out for the day. The parent with OCPD is likely to have a very strict schedule they have to adhere to. They will likely become angry or caustic when that schedule is altered for any reason. In this case, the OCPD patient becomes preoccupied with ensuring everything goes according to schedule and misses the point of why they spend the day out, which is to spend and enjoy time with their child. Such is a common occurrence for those with OCPD.

2. Requiring Perfection

Another symptom of OCPD is a self-imposed requirement for perfectionism. This need for perfectionism can interfere with the OCPD patient's completion of a task in both their professional and personal lives. The OCPD patient will simply refuse to move past small and unimportant details in an effort to complete a task. This can show itself in trivial tasks, such as folding towels, where the patient may refuse to move on to the next task until the towel is folded exactly to their standard. A more problematic example would be refusal of an OCPD patient to turn in a report until they double and triple check the document to ensure that every comma is used in a correct manner, causing them to become late in the submission of the said report.

3. Overly Devoted to Work

Excessive devotion to work is also a commonly recognized symptom of OCPD. This devotion goes beyond the typical of even the best workers and has a negative impact on the individual's personal life. Birthdays, holidays, and anniversaries are often overlooked by the OCPD in favor of working, even if there is no economic necessity to do so. The OCPD patient will most likely perceive observing and celebrating such holidays, instead of working, in a negative light. Moreover, if they are pressured to skip work to spend time observing these occasions, the patient will likely experience stress as a result. They are unlikely to focus on the moment at hand in such a scenario. Instead, they will be preoccupied about the work they should supposedly be completing at that time. It is no surprise that this can have a negative impact on the relationships of the OCPD patient. Although it is possible for the OCPD patients to have friendly or romantic relationships, such relationships will be difficult to maintain.

4. Rigid Views of Morality

Those with OCPD tend to have an overly developed sense of conscientiousness. The OCPD patient tends to view matters of morality in an extremely black and white manner, with little understanding or compassion toward those who commit acts outside the patient's view of what is 'right'. Ethics and values, as defined by the patient, are very important to these individuals and can be a core aspect of their character. They are often inflexible with regards to these views and have a tendency to superimpose their own sense of morals onto others. This typically makes those with OCPD very honest and hardworking individuals. It can also, however, alienate them from those who disagree with their values. If they are not careful, it could even have a negative impact on their life.

5. Hoarding

OCPD has also been linked with hoarding. Hoarding may be an indicator that the patient has OCPD. The OCPD patient finds it difficult to discard items even when those items no longer serve its purpose. This goes beyond items which may have sentimental value and applies to what others would identify as rubbish. To those with OCPD, relinquishing these items may be very difficult. Their fears cause them difficulty. They think that they might need this item in the future and not have it. This fear is not entirely rational as the more logical argument is that they can simply buy a replacement for the item should they need it again. However, this more rational reasoning will often fall on deaf ears.

6. Reluctance to Delegate

OCPD patients have a tendency to dislike delegating tasks to others. The high expectation of the OCPD patient is difficult, if not impossible, for others to meet. The OCPD patient will not settle for a task that does not meet their expectations. This causes the patient to be reluctant in delegating tasks, which they believe to be of utmost importance to others. Even if they do delegate such tasks, they may re-do the work if they feel that it does not meet their standards. This is applicable to everything, from the manner in which a spouse folds the laundry to the way a coworker completes a project. This obsession with meeting standards may ultimately result in tension rising from relationships. In the end, those with OCPD may prefer to work alone rather than risk working with others who do not abide by their rigid standard of doing things.

7. Tight-Fisted Spending Style

Those with OCPD feel uncomfortable about spending money. The OCPD patient is frequently a person who resents spending money on anyone or anything, including themselves. Rather than seeing money as a tool to gain what they want, those with OCPD usually believe in hoarding their wealth in the event of some future catastrophe. While this trait is not something alarming when found in mild forms or in the general population, those with OCPD take this to the extreme. They may resent spending money on basic necessities or exhibit resentment toward those who spend on their behalf. Birthdays and Christmas, for example, may cause resentment or stress on the part of an OCPD patient which may not be found in others.

8. Extreme Stubbornness

The OCPD patient is typically a very rigid and stubborn individual. It is very difficult to convince those with OCPD that they are incorrect in any manner. In fact, this symptom may cause the patient to deny that they might have a disorder in the first place. They are also unwilling to entertain the ideas of others especially if those ideas conflict with theirs. This can cause significant problems to the patient as this might cause others to negatively react about having their ideas dismissed by the OCPD patient. Another example would be their resistance to the adoption of new technologies. The OCPD patient is unwilling to use new technology to complete a task even if that technology makes the task simpler and be accomplished much faster. Taking a different route to work using debit or credit cards rather than cash and other similar behaviors can indicate a level of rigidity that is typical of an OCPD patient.

9. Need for Order

Those with OCPD have an overwhelming need for order in their lives. Most symptoms can be seen as a result of the need for order in the patient's life. Order and organization allows those with OCPD to have control in their lives. The lack of order creates feelings of overwhelming stress and anxiety in the OCPD patient. In the context of the environmental cause for OCPD, this may be a reaction to the lack of control the patient felt as a child in a traumatic situation. Order is something that brings those with OCPD a measure of peace, although they are unlikely to recognize it as such. Like other symptoms of OCPD, this symptom is stronger than those found in typical individuals and may have negative consequences. The patient's need for order may place a strain on a marriage with a less organized partner. Similarly, this need may have negative consequences to the patient when they find themselves in less orderly surroundings.

Seven Common Therapy Methods for Obsessive Compulsive Personality Disorder

There are several different therapy methods for OCPD and each of these has both positive and negative aspects. Ultimately, it is up to the patient, their families, and their health care providers to decide which treatment, and the intensity of that treatment, will work best for the patient. It is important to remember that the selection of a treatment method should only be made after consulting with a qualified professional who can help the patient make the best well-informed decision.

1. Psychotherapy

Psychotherapy is a therapeutic treatment based on talk therapy. A psychologist or psychiatrist develops a relationship with the patient and attempts to guide the patient towards a more healthy mental state. In the case of OCPD, this therapy is typically aimed at the short-term relief of symptoms than on the long-term alteration of the patient's personality. This is due to the difficulty in altering a person's nature, which is often beyond the skills of the clinician. It is also unlikely that the patient will be willing to, or able to, pay for such a long-term treatment. This is especially true in light of the fact that, due to their highly stubborn nature, it is exceedingly difficult to change the OCPD patient's nature.

Therapy focuses on having the patients learn how to properly identify and realize their emotions. Most people diagnosed with OCPD are more in-tune with their thoughts, rather than their emotions. They may become so focused on their thoughts that they are completely unaware of the emotions they are experiencing. They can frequently have problems recalling what their emotions were during an experience, while they may recall exactly what they were thinking. Altering this pattern can have a noticeable and significant improvement for those with OCPD.

2. Hospitalization

Hospitalization of those with OCPD is relatively rare and usually unnecessary. The nature of their disorder does not regularly impact the daily lives of OCPD patients and does not typically represent a threat to the patient, or to others. However, there are instances wherein the patient experiences some extreme life event or stressor which triggers their disorder to the extent that it causes a significant impact in their ability to complete daily tasks. In this case, hospitalization may be necessary. Likewise, instances wherein the patient becomes paralyzed by their disorder, such as being unable to leave their bed or to stop their compulsive behavior, may require hospitalization. Thankfully, these instances are uncommon. What is important to note about hospitalization is that it is not a functional long-term treatment option for OCPD. While it is a viable way to address immediate short-term and severe issues, a longer treatment method will be necessary for the patient's management.

3. Medications

Medication is not the treatment option most psychiatrists would prescribe for those with OCPD. Medications can carry with them serious side-effects and there is also the possibility of a patient becoming dependent on the drug. However, in instances wherein the patient's daily life is being severely affected by OCPD but not severe enough to warrant hospitalization, medication may be a viable option. Medications have recently been improved by the development of drugs, such as Prozac, which have showed some symptom relief for those with OCPD. This indicates that these drugs could provide some measure of relief for those suffering from OCPD. This method, however, will only relieve symptoms and not treat the underlying disorder. Therefore, medication may be a viable short-term option for treatment. However, it should be replaced, as soon as possible, with a method better suited for the long-term.

4. Cognitive Therapy

Cognitive therapy is a form of psychotherapy that was developed by an American psychiatrist named Aaron T. Beck. Cognitive therapy is focused on the psychiatrist and patient working collaboratively to recognize and alter unhealthy or illogical thought patterns. Cognitive therapy focuses on testing unsound thought processes to help the patient realize the error of their thinking, and to eventually alter the patient's thinking pattern in a natural way. In the treatment for OCPD, cognitive therapy is more focused on managing the reaction of patients to the thoughts they have and not in stopping the thoughts themselves. This is a more manageable task for both the therapist and the patient and can alleviate the symptoms the patient experiences due to their disorder. Cognitive therapy is a good long-term solution for OCPD patients that can have a positive and long-lasting effect on their behavior. The negative aspect to this therapy is the relatively long treatment time needed and the cost for such enduring treatment. Pursuing this therapy for extended periods may be impossible for those with a limited amount of resources or a less than generous health insurance plan.

5. Support Groups

Support groups are readily available for those with OCPD and their loved ones. These groups can be found in local communities or online, depending on the preference of the patient and their location. As a treatment option, support groups are a mid-level option. Some patients may not be affected much by their OCPD. Thus, joining the support group might be the only treatment needed. However, patients who are more significantly affected by their disorder may need additional therapy in conjunction with the support group sessions. Nevertheless, joining a support group is highly recommended. Patients can find a valuable source of support there as well as be introduced to positive treatments or providers. They can also learn more about their disorder and gain an understanding of their condition from someone other than their health care provider. A simple web search will turn up many groups that patients may join, including *www.ocpd.freeforums.org* and *www.obsessive-compulsive-personality-disorder.meetup.com*. Both are free forums for those who suffer from OCPD and have a loved one who has OCPD.

6. Relaxation Techniques

The patient with OCPD is someone who is bombarded with stressors. They experience high levels of tension and anxiety which contribute to the aggravation of their disorder. Relieving some of this tension and anxiety can help the patient re-assert some measure of self-control over themselves and their disorder. It may also provide the patient with a chance to judge their compulsion from a more rational viewpoint, and possibly even rejecting that compulsion. In order for this to be possible, the patient may use relaxation techniques to help alleviate the tension they feel.

Relaxation techniques may include specific breathing techniques or even yoga poses, which fosters a sense of serenity in the patient and allows them to think past the immediate moment. The negative aspect to this treatment method is that the underlying disorder is, likewise, not treated. This means that while the patient may gain some measure of control over their compulsions if consistently applied, relaxation techniques will never end the compulsions themselves. The positive aspect of this treatment method, aside from the immediate relief provided, is that there is little to no real cost accrued when utilizing these techniques. There are multiple sources from which to learn the best techniques for a specific individual, such as those found online or at the local library. Another major benefit is that this treatment option can be utilized in real time. Whenever the patient begins to experience stress from their compulsive thoughts, he or she can make him or herself calm down and manage the symptoms. This is very much unlike other therapies which require a therapist, a pill, or some other secondary device for it to work.

7. Aromatherapy

Aromatherapy may seem like an odd treatment choice for OCPD. However, much like relaxation techniques, aromatherapy can help to relieve tension and stress induced by the patient's OCPD. Aromatherapy can be administered in a variety of ways, such as through massage with essential oils, and aromatic baths or vaporization. Certain oils and scents are used to provide relief for certain symptoms. Lavender, sandalwood, and nutmeg, for example, are all used to help alleviate stress. Vanilla, orange blossom, chamomile, and other floral scents are used to help relieve anxiety. Certain aromas may be better for some individuals than for others and each patient should find a combination that works best for them. The benefits of aromatherapy are very helpful in the relief of the symptoms experienced by a person with OCPD. However, like many other treatment options, aromatherapy is not a cure for the patient's OCPD and may need to be used in conjunction with other treatments.

How to Choose the Right Therapy

OCPD may vary in intensity, from being a mild personality quirk that the patient and others learn to live with, to being a true challenge to the patient. OCPD is unique in nature in such a way that while these individuals experience difficulty as a result of their disorder, many of them lead relatively normal lives unabated. Individuals with OCPD can have successful careers, marry, have children, and enjoy friendships.

This variation is an important element in determining the right therapy. If the patient has a lower level version of OCPD, lighter treatment options may be better than high-handed tactics, such as medication or psychotherapy. Likewise, a patient with a severe case of OCPD that affects their day to day lifestyle is unlikely to gain lasting benefits from just joining a support group. More intense treatment methods may be in order for these patients, such as cognitive

43

therapy. The first step in selecting the correct therapy for the patient, therefore, is to determine the intensity of therapy needed. Determining which level of treatment is best for the patient will require the help of a licensed professional who can bring an informed opinion as well as an unbiased view to the selection process.

After determining the intensity of treatment necessary with the help of a licensed professional, patients should research on their treatment options. Having an in-depth understanding of what a treatment requires, and what benefits and costs come with it, is an essential part of choosing the right therapy. A lack of knowledge can lead to serious mistakes in choosing the best therapy. For instance, a person who is unaware of the limitations of medication in treating OCPD may believe a prescription will 'cure' them. Finding out differently later in the treatment process can cause undue stress that may trigger greater symptoms from their disorder. While a professional health care provider such as a psychiatrist or psychologist can make recommendations regarding treatment, the patient is ultimately the only one capable of making that decision. Therefore, patients should be well-informed as possible on all treatment options before selecting the treatment path they wish to take.

In addition to determining the level of intensity the patient will require in their therapy and researching the treatment options available to them, patients should be aware of their individual preferences and realities. For example, if a patient is unwilling or unsuitable to learn and implement breathing techniques, the patient should focus on options that appeal to them more. There is little use in spending time and money on a treatment option that the patient feels uncomfortable with as they are unlikely to utilize it over the long term. On the other hand, focusing on those therapies which appeal to the patient the most will encourage the actual use of that therapy. Those who are interested in natural treatment methods may do better with aromatherapy, for instance, rather than with medications and vice versa.

This is not to say that choosing one therapy excludes another. Due to the type of therapies available to help treat OCPD, many treatment options can be used in combination with others to provide the best results. Those who opt for cognitive or psychotherapy treatments may also benefit from breathing techniques and aromatherapies. Regardless of the other chosen treatment methods, patients would also do well to join a support group. Joining such a group can have a very positive influence on the patient's outlook on their disorder while having a sense of belongingness and community. These and other combinations of treatment options should be discussed with the patient's health care provider. They may even create a treatment program guide that includes each of the options selected, including when and how to use them. This will provide the patient with a semblance of control that the OCPD patient needs to feel comfortable, while also providing valuable knowledge in an easy to access format.

This combination is not only for those treatment options which are less medical in nature. Psychotherapy or cognitive therapy may both use medications, if necessary, to help the patient overcome difficult periods in their treatment. Hospitalization can also be utilized, if absolutely necessary, in conjunction with the other therapy methods.

Once the patient has selected the treatment option he or she would like to utilize, he or she should begin to research on potential providers for those treatments. While the patient is likely to have at least one mental health provider, the patient may want one or more additional providers to obtain access to less traditional forms of therapy. If this is the case, patients should first ask for a recommendation from their current mental health care provider. Most psychologists or psychiatrists will have a readily available list of providers with whom they associate with that may be able to provide different treatment options.

Even if the patient's current provider has such a list, patients should research on each name given to them before selecting. Checking each doctor's credentials, degrees, and reviews is a great step to take. Patients should also check the experience of each provider in working with OCPD patients. This should eliminate some of the providers the patient is considering. Scheduling an office visit with different care providers allows the patient to gauge the different styles and personalities of those whom they may be receiving treatment from. Patients should eliminate from the list those whom they feel uncomfortable with, or those who have a different treatment plan from what the patient has in mind.

The most important aspect of selecting a therapy, or therapies, is creating a combination of factors that allows the patient to live a normal life as possible. Selecting that combination should always be done with the consideration of the patient's lifestyle, personality type (aside from their disorder), preferences, and resources. Patients should feel comfortable with their health care providers and be at ease with the therapies they choose. As long as those requirements are met, the patient will be able to select the best therapy and the best provider for their needs.

How to Overcome Obsessive Compulsive Personality Disorder

Overcoming OCPD may seem a daunting task for both the patient and for their loved ones. OCPD is a disorder that, in many ways, becomes the defining characteristic of the patient. OCPD patients may not know who they would be without this aspect of their personality, and frankly, many may be afraid to find out. However, for those who can see the problems OCPD creates for them, and for those who are brave enough to address them, OCPD is a manageable task. The keyword here is manageable. Overcoming a disorder as all-encompassing as OCPD is neither an easy task, nor is it a fast thing to do. Patients should be prepared for long-term treatment and lifestyle changes.

In order to overcome OCPD, patients must take several important steps. Recognizing that they have a problem to begin with is the first and, perhaps, most difficult step for OCPD patients. Most OCPD patients do not see a problem with their current lifestyle and they are reluctant to dramatically alter a fundamental part of their life. The reality is that OCPD does affect the life of a patient in a negative way. Many people with OCPD are missing out on essential parts of their life. They often fail to enjoy what little time they spend with their family. Furthermore, they may strain personal relationships or even damage their careers as a result of their OCPD.

The OCPD patient, however, often overlooks these negative aspects of their current lifestyle. When they do see these less than perfect situations arise, they may blame others or circumstances rather than see any problem with themselves. Patients should ask themselves the following questions to recognize that they have a disorder:

1. Do they allow their need for order and perfection to derail projects?

2. Do they become so engrossed in staying on schedule that they forget to enjoy their activities?

3. Does working through holidays, even when they do not have to, a common occurrence?

4. Are they reluctant to allow others to complete tasks for fear that it would not be done 'correctly'?

5. Can they remember the last time they truly appreciated how something made them feel?

Once the patient begins to accept that they have a problem, their next step is to seek out a professional mental health care provider. This professional, who should either be a licensed psychologist or licensed psychiatrist, will be able to formally diagnose the patient. It is important to remember that diagnosing or treating a disorder without the aid of a professional is dangerous and potentially costly. A person who fails to seek the aid of a mental health professional and yet proceeds to treat their disorder will most likely do harm to their self or spend thousands without seeing results. Enlisting the aid of a qualified mental health professional can prevent both outcomes.

The professional will be able to help the patient in more ways than just providing a correct diagnosis. They may be able to offer their own services and a treatment method depending on their skill set and experience level. Even if the patient's original provider is not capable of providing the needed treatment itself, they are likely to recommend others who will be able to do so. These providers will also be able to give the patient much needed information about their disorder as well as how to join a support group. Likewise they will be able to present what treatment options are available for the patient and what each of these options entail. The most critical aspect of this step is ensuring that the patient chooses the right provider for them. Researching before selecting the provider is a smart idea. Patients should check for education levels, awards and certifications, patient reviews, and experience levels with OCPD before choosing their provider.

After enlisting the aid of a professional, OCPD patients should enlist the aid of family and friends. A personality disorder is something that does not only affect the patient but everyone around the patient as well. Likewise, treating a personality disorder takes more than just the effort of the patient but the effort of all those involved in the patient's life. Family members and friends can be valuable resources in battling OCPD. As the people closest to the patient, they are even more likely to recognize areas wherein the patient's disorder affects them more than the patient themselves. Speaking to those closest to them can help the OCPD patient understand what areas of their life they truly need to focus their treatment on. Likewise, it shall give the patient a sense of community and support in their effort to change themselves.

Moreover, these individuals can act as real-time alerts to the patient's disorder, giving the patient a perspective on their actions at the moment. This allows the patient to choose their behavior in a meaningful way. For instance, if a child informs their OCPD parent on a family outing that the parent is becoming overly caught in keeping things on schedule and not focusing on enjoying the family, the patient may be able to make a conscious choice to alter their behavior. This also allows those around the patient to gain an understanding of their behavior, potentially reducing the frustration they feel as a result of the patient's OCPD and hopefully improving the relationship.

Once the patient has spoken to his or her family, they should begin the treatment or treatments of their choice. The important element to this step in OCPD is realizing that the patient cannot overcome their disorder by themselves. Those with OCPD have a marked tendency to be both stubborn and loners by nature. This combination may lead the OCPD patient to draw the false conclusion that they can address their disorder without taking any of the treatment options available to them. This could not be more wrong. OCPD is not something that a patient can overcome by themselves. The patient will most likely not recognize when and how their disorder affects them. Treating their disorder effectively is way beyond the capability of most patients. Therefore, external help is absolutely necessary for the OCPD patient to overcome their disorder.

Not every patient needs the same type of treatment. Patients should utilize the opinion of their professional provider, closest family and friends, and their own good judgment to select the treatment option best for them. In addition to any treatment option the patient chooses, it would be a wise decision for both the patient and their family to join a support group. Joining a support group offers many great benefits to the patient and their family, including priceless information, a steady source of support, and a judgment free avenue to voice out frustrations that arise due to either the OCPD or the treatment thereof. There is little to no downside in joining these groups as they are generally free of cost and can be accessed either in person or online. Utilizing such a useful tool in addition to other treatment options may greatly contribute to a patient's success in managing their OCPD.

Overall, overcoming OCPD revolves around many different, yet equally important, elements, such as the patient's recognition of their disorder and their willingness to address this disorder, the help of a reliable and experienced professional in both diagnosing and treating the patient's disorder, the support of the patient's family and friends who will act as safeguards against old habits while supporting positive changes, and the utilization of the best treatment options available to the patient, including as many different avenues of treatment as necessary.

These elements work together to give the OCPD patient a formidable toolbox with four essential tools in managing their disorder. The patient's recognition of their disorder gives them awareness that they become cognizant of the underlying causes for their behavior. By seeking professional help, patients gain knowledge that they can utilize to make smart decisions in managing their disorder. Relying on friends and family provides the patient with a foundation of support to help them make the necessary decisions and changes in their lives needed to address their OCPD. Seeking treatment is a concrete action that will provide the patient with concrete results in managing their OCPD. These four tools (awareness, knowledge, support, and action) are all that the patient needs to successfully manage their disorder.

However, it is unlikely that a patient will be completely 'cured' of their OCPD even with intensive treatment. Patients will likely always experience compulsions due to their OCPD. What the OCPD patient should remember is that the ultimate goal in addressing their disorder is not to be 'fixed', but to enable the patient to live a normal life as possible. With the help of these critical elements, the patient should be able to effectively manage their OCPD impulses and live a more normal life.

How to Find Your Escape

Those with OCPD are always thinking about the next step they should take and the 'what ifs' in life. These patients seek to control their own future by imposing strict rules and high expectations on themselves and on those around them. Moreover, these patients are so wrapped up in their thoughts that they are often completely unaware of their feelings. Therefore, finding an escape for those with OCPD is about learning to appreciate the present moment for what it is and recognizing the feelings which they have at that moment.

To recognize the feelings that a patient have at the moment, they must first be present in the moment. This may seem like an easy solution to such a difficult problem. However, learning to truly appreciate the present moment is a challenging task than many would believe. For those with OCPD, focusing at the present is not something natural to them. Their minds are already far ahead on the next task, problem, or program. Learning to focus on the present takes a great deal of conscious thought and concentration. However, it can be accomplished with a few simple skills.

One skill is the ability to focus on something outside of your own mind. If you are listening to (and singing along with) a song, try to focus on every word of the lyrics so that you are actively aware of what you are singing along to. The same goes for watching a movie or a play. Concentrate on listening to the dialogue and the appreciation of the scenery. Another way to focus on the present is through the practice of breathing techniques. Concentrating on your breathing pattern and ignoring everything else allows a person to ignore distractions that generate stress. Patients should also limit their attempts at multi-tasking. Patients are unable to truly concentrate and enjoy a single task if they do it.

Once the patient has learned how to be present in the moment, they should begin the journey of recognizing their own feelings. To others, this may sound slightly odd. Recognizing our emotions is something that most of us do without conscious effort. Those with OCPD, however, are so consumed by their thoughts that they often fail to recognize or recall their emotions in any given moment. This is a critical failure in the patient's ability to escape from their disorder, as the patient who does not recognize their own emotions cannot enjoy them.

To begin appreciating their own emotions, patients should begin to keep an 'emotion log'. This is a journal where the patient can write down their emotions as they experience them, without regard as to the positive or negative nature of those emotions. The important thing is that the patient consciously focuses on their emotions rather than on their thoughts and cements those feelings in a tangible way by writing them down. This teaches the patient to focus more on their present activities and the feelings these activities create in them, rather than allow themselves to focus on negative thoughts or unnecessary worries.

Escape for those with OCPD is about letting go of their disorder for even a single moment so that they can truly enjoy their lives. Happiness, fun, and laughter are the things that allow us to find solace in the day to day stresses of life. Those with OCPD have a difficult time than most people to recognize and enjoy emotions. By learning to live in the moment and to recognize their own feelings, those with OCPD can enjoy the same relief as the rest of us do, and find an escape from their OCPD.

Conclusion

OCPD is a mental health condition that is characterized by a preoccupation with rules, order, organization and control. Those who suffer from OCPD are often unaware that they have a problem as this disorder integrates itself into the patient's personality. These patients display a range of symptoms, including an overly zealous devotion to work, an excessive need for order, a penchant for hoarding, and reluctance to delegate tasks, among others. The symptoms of this disorder cause the patient a great deal of personal stress and places undue strains on the patient's interpersonal relationships.

OCPD includes five subtypes, each with its specific and unique predispositions in personality. These subtypes are knowns as the conscientious compulsive, the bureaucratic compulsive, the parsimonious compulsive, the puritanical compulsive, and the bedeviled compulsive. While each of these subtypes

64

display their disorder in unique ways, all share a compulsive need for order and an extremely high expectation of themselves and others. These unreasonable expectations can negatively impact the patient's life and state of mind, resulting in the need for treatment.

An OCPD patient may choose from different treatment options with the help of a qualified professional. These treatment options include psychotherapy, medication, aromatherapy, cognitive therapy, and more. Many of these treatment methods can be combined to give the patient a greater chance for success in managing their disorder. Patients must come to terms with the fact that they must manage their disorder and that a complete eradication of OCPD is highly unlikely. However, with enough effort, proper treatment, professional help, and support from the family, the OCPD patient can successfully manage their disorder and live a happy and well-adjusted life.

Final Word/About the Author

I was born and raised in Norwalk, Connecticut. Growing up, I could often be found spending afternoons reading in the local public library about management techniques and leadership styles, along with overall outlooks towards life. It was from spending those afternoons reading about how others have led productive lives that I was inspired to start studying patterns of human behavior and self-improvement. Usually I write works around sports to learn more about influential athletes in the hopes that from my writing, you the reader can walk away inspired to put in an equal if not greater amount of hard work and perseverance to pursue your goals. However, I began writing about psychology topics such as Obsessive Compulsive Personality disorder so that I could help others better understand why they act and think the way they do and how to build on their strengths while also identifying their weaknesses. If you enjoyed *Obsessive Compulsive Personality Disorder: The Ultimate Guide to Symptoms, Treatment and Prevention* please leave a review! Also, you can read more of my general works on *Best Places to Retire: The Top 15 Affordable Towns for Retirement in Asia, Best Places to Retire: The Top 15 Affordable Towns for Retirement in Europe, Best Places to Retire: The Top 15 Affordable Towns for Retirement in Florida, Best Places to Retire: The Top 15 Affordable Towns for Retirement on a Budget, Gratitude, How to Fundraise, How to Get Out of the Friend Zone, Histrionic Personality Disorder, Narcissistic Personality Disorder, Avoidant Personality Disorder, Sundown Syndrome, ISTJs, ISFJs, ISFPs, INTJs, INFPs, INFJs, ESFPs, ESFJs, ESTJs, ENFPs, ENFJs, ENTJs, How to be Witty, How to be Likeable, How to be Creative, Bargain Shopping, Productivity Hacks, Morning Meditation, Becoming a Father,* and *33 Life*

Lessons: Success Principles, Career Advice & Habits of Successful People in the Kindle Store.

Like what you read?

I write because I love sharing personal development information on topics like why people behave the way they do with fantastic readers like you. My readers inspire me to write more so please do not hesitate to let me know what you thought by leaving a review! If you love books on life, basketball, or productivity, check out my website at claytongeoffreys.com to join my exclusive list where I let you know about my latest books. Aside from being the first to hear about my latest releases, you can also download a free copy of _33 Life Lessons: Success Principles, Career Advice & Habits of Successful People_. See you there!

33 LIFE LESSONS

SUCCESS PRINCIPLES, CAREER ADVICE
& HABITS OF SUCCESSFUL PEOPLE

CLAYTON GEOFFREYS

Printed in Great Britain
by Amazon

37899432R00046